50 Beach Dishes for Partying

By: Kelly Johnson

Table of Contents

- Grilled Shrimp Skewers
- Fish Tacos with Mango Salsa
- Tropical Fruit Salad
- Guacamole with Tortilla Chips
- Coconut Shrimp with Sweet Chili Sauce
- Chicken Skewers with Peanut Sauce
- Spinach and Artichoke Dip
- Tuna Poke Bowls
- Veggie and Hummus Platter
- Grilled Corn on the Cob with Lime and Chili
- Shrimp Cocktail with Cocktail Sauce
- Watermelon and Feta Salad
- Crab Cakes with Remoulade Sauce
- Caprese Salad Skewers
- Grilled Veggie Kebabs
- Pineapple Salsa with Tortilla Chips
- Pulled Pork Sliders
- Guava BBQ Chicken Wings
- Cucumber and Cream Cheese Sandwiches
- Roasted Red Pepper and Goat Cheese Dip
- Hawaiian BBQ Pork Tacos
- Mini Fish and Chips Bites
- Chips and Salsa
- Shrimp Ceviche
- Grilled Zucchini and Squash
- Chicken Caesar Salad Wraps
- Fresh Fruit Skewers
- Bacon-Wrapped Dates
- Beef Sliders with Pickles
- Spicy Tuna Tartare
- Chips and Guacamole Stuffed Avocados
- Grilled Pineapple with Brown Sugar
- Bruschetta with Tomato and Basil
- Lobster Roll Sliders
- Veggie Spring Rolls with Peanut Dipping Sauce

- Crab Dip with Crackers
- Mahi-Mahi Tacos with Slaw
- BBQ Chicken Drumsticks
- Baked Mozzarella Sticks
- Pita Bread with Baba Ganoush
- Stuffed Mushrooms
- Poke Nachos
- Salmon Croquettes
- Sweet Potato Fries with Ketchup
- Margarita Shrimp Salad
- Cold Shrimp Salad with Dill and Lemon
- Baked Brie with Fig Jam
- Grilled Asparagus with Balsamic Glaze
- Tofu Skewers with Soy Sauce
- Lemon and Herb Marinated Olives

Grilled Shrimp Skewers

Ingredients:

- 1 lb large shrimp, peeled and deveined
- 2 tablespoons olive oil
- 2 tablespoons fresh lemon juice
- 2 cloves garlic, minced
- 1 teaspoon paprika
- 1 teaspoon cumin
- Salt and pepper to taste
- Fresh parsley for garnish

Instructions:

1. **Prepare the Marinade:**
    - In a bowl, combine olive oil, lemon juice, garlic, paprika, cumin, salt, and pepper.
2. **Marinate the Shrimp:**
    - Place the shrimp in the marinade and toss to coat. Let them marinate for at least 30 minutes in the refrigerator.
3. **Grill the Shrimp:**
    - Preheat the grill to medium-high heat. Thread the shrimp onto skewers. Grill for 2-3 minutes per side, until the shrimp are pink and opaque.
4. **Serve:**
    - Garnish with fresh parsley and serve immediately with a side of rice or salad.

Fish Tacos with Mango Salsa

Ingredients:

- 1 lb white fish fillets (such as tilapia or cod)
- 1 tablespoon olive oil
- 1 teaspoon cumin
- 1 teaspoon chili powder
- Salt and pepper to taste
- 8 small corn tortillas
- 1 ripe mango, diced
- 1/4 cup red onion, finely chopped
- 1/4 cup cilantro, chopped
- 1 tablespoon lime juice
- 1 jalapeño, finely chopped (optional)

Instructions:

1. **Cook the Fish:**
    - Season the fish fillets with olive oil, cumin, chili powder, salt, and pepper. Heat a skillet over medium heat and cook the fish for 3-4 minutes per side until flaky.
2. **Make the Mango Salsa:**
    - In a bowl, combine the mango, red onion, cilantro, lime juice, and jalapeño. Mix well.
3. **Assemble the Tacos:**
    - Warm the tortillas in a dry skillet. Flake the cooked fish and divide among the tortillas. Top with mango salsa.
4. **Serve:**
    - Serve the tacos with a side of avocado or sour cream.

Tropical Fruit Salad

Ingredients:

- 1 mango, peeled and diced
- 1 pineapple, peeled, cored, and diced
- 2 kiwis, peeled and sliced
- 1/2 papaya, peeled and diced
- 1/2 cup coconut flakes (unsweetened)
- 1 tablespoon fresh mint, chopped
- 2 tablespoons honey or agave syrup
- Juice of 1 lime

Instructions:

1. **Prepare the Fruit:**
    - In a large bowl, combine all the diced fruit (mango, pineapple, kiwi, and papaya).
2. **Add the Coconut and Mint:**
    - Sprinkle the coconut flakes and chopped mint over the fruit.
3. **Dress the Salad:**
    - Drizzle honey and lime juice over the fruit salad and toss gently to combine.
4. **Serve:**
    - Serve chilled, as a refreshing side or dessert.

Guacamole with Tortilla Chips

Ingredients:

- 3 ripe avocados, peeled and pitted
- 1/2 red onion, finely chopped
- 1 jalapeño, deseeded and chopped
- 1/4 cup cilantro, chopped
- Juice of 2 limes
- Salt and pepper to taste
- Tortilla chips for dipping

Instructions:

1. **Mash the Avocados:**
    - In a bowl, mash the avocados with a fork until smooth, but still a bit chunky.
2. **Add the Ingredients:**
    - Add red onion, jalapeño, cilantro, lime juice, salt, and pepper. Mix well.
3. **Serve:**
    - Serve immediately with tortilla chips for dipping.

Coconut Shrimp with Sweet Chili Sauce

Ingredients:

For the Coconut Shrimp:

- 1 lb large shrimp, peeled and deveined
- 1/2 cup all-purpose flour
- 2 large eggs, beaten
- 1 cup shredded coconut (sweetened or unsweetened, depending on preference)
- 1/2 cup panko breadcrumbs
- 1/2 teaspoon salt
- 1/4 teaspoon black pepper
- Vegetable oil, for frying

For the Sweet Chili Sauce:

- 1/2 cup sweet chili sauce (store-bought or homemade)
- 1 tablespoon rice vinegar
- 1 teaspoon lime juice
- 1/2 teaspoon soy sauce (optional)

Instructions:

1. Prepare the Shrimp:

- In a shallow bowl, place the flour.
- In a second shallow bowl, beat the eggs.
- In a third shallow bowl, mix the shredded coconut, panko breadcrumbs, salt, and pepper.

2. Coat the Shrimp:

- Dip each shrimp first into the flour, coating it evenly.
- Then dip it into the beaten egg, ensuring it is fully coated.
- Finally, dredge the shrimp in the coconut-breadcrumb mixture, pressing gently to adhere.

3. Fry the Shrimp:

- Heat about 1/2 inch of vegetable oil in a large skillet over medium-high heat.

- Once the oil is hot, carefully add the shrimp in batches. Fry the shrimp for 2-3 minutes per side, or until golden brown and crispy.
- Remove the shrimp from the skillet and place them on a paper towel-lined plate to drain excess oil.

4. Prepare the Sweet Chili Sauce:

- In a small bowl, mix together the sweet chili sauce, rice vinegar, lime juice, and soy sauce (if using).
- Stir until well combined. Taste and adjust the sweetness or tanginess as needed.

5. Serve:

- Arrange the coconut shrimp on a plate and serve with the sweet chili sauce on the side for dipping.

Chicken Skewers with Peanut Sauce

Ingredients:

- 1 lb chicken breast, cut into 1-inch cubes
- 2 tablespoons olive oil
- 1 tablespoon soy sauce
- 1 tablespoon honey
- 1 teaspoon garlic powder
- 1 teaspoon ginger powder
- 1/4 teaspoon cayenne pepper
- 1/4 cup peanut butter
- 2 tablespoons soy sauce
- 1 tablespoon lime juice
- 1 tablespoon honey
- 1/4 cup coconut milk
- 1 tablespoon sesame oil

Instructions:

1. **Marinate the Chicken:**
    - In a bowl, combine olive oil, soy sauce, honey, garlic powder, ginger, cayenne, salt, and pepper. Add the chicken cubes and marinate for at least 30 minutes.
2. **Prepare the Peanut Sauce:**
    - In a separate bowl, whisk together peanut butter, soy sauce, lime juice, honey, coconut milk, and sesame oil until smooth.
3. **Grill the Chicken:**
    - Thread the marinated chicken onto skewers. Grill over medium-high heat for 5-6 minutes per side until cooked through.
4. **Serve:**
    - Serve the chicken skewers with peanut sauce for dipping.

Spinach and Artichoke Dip

Ingredients:

- 1 (14 oz) can artichoke hearts, drained and chopped
- 4 cups fresh spinach, chopped
- 1 cup cream cheese, softened
- 1/2 cup sour cream
- 1/2 cup mayonnaise
- 1 cup Parmesan cheese, grated
- 1 cup mozzarella cheese, shredded
- 2 cloves garlic, minced
- Salt and pepper to taste

Instructions:

1. **Sauté the Spinach:**
     - In a skillet, sauté the spinach and garlic until wilted and fragrant (about 3-4 minutes).
2. **Prepare the Dip:**
     - In a bowl, combine cream cheese, sour cream, mayonnaise, Parmesan, and mozzarella. Stir in the artichokes and sautéed spinach.
3. **Bake the Dip:**
     - Preheat the oven to 375°F (190°C). Transfer the dip to a baking dish and bake for 20-25 minutes until golden and bubbly.
4. **Serve:**
     - Serve with crackers, pita bread, or vegetable sticks.

Tuna Poke Bowls

Ingredients:

- 1 lb sushi-grade tuna, diced
- 1 tablespoon soy sauce
- 1 tablespoon sesame oil
- 1 tablespoon rice vinegar
- 1/2 teaspoon ginger, grated
- 1 avocado, sliced
- 1/2 cucumber, thinly sliced
- 1/2 cup edamame, cooked
- 1/4 cup sesame seeds
- Cooked rice for serving

Instructions:

1. **Marinate the Tuna:**
   - In a bowl, combine tuna, soy sauce, sesame oil, rice vinegar, and grated ginger. Let it marinate for 15-20 minutes.
2. **Assemble the Bowls:**
   - Serve the marinated tuna over a bowl of cooked rice. Top with avocado, cucumber, edamame, and sesame seeds.
3. **Serve:**
   - Drizzle with extra soy sauce or sesame oil if desired.

Veggie and Hummus Platter

Ingredients:

- 1 cup hummus (store-bought or homemade)
- 1 cucumber, sliced
- 1 carrot, cut into sticks
- 1 bell pepper, sliced
- 1/2 cup cherry tomatoes
- 1/4 cup olives
- Fresh parsley for garnish

Instructions:

1. **Prepare the Vegetables:**
    - Arrange the cucumber, carrot sticks, bell pepper slices, cherry tomatoes, and olives on a platter.
2. **Serve:**
    - Serve with a bowl of hummus in the center for dipping. Garnish with fresh parsley.

Grilled Corn on the Cob with Lime and Chili

Ingredients:

- 4 ears of corn, husked
- 2 tablespoons butter, melted
- 1 teaspoon chili powder
- Juice of 1 lime
- Salt and pepper to taste
- Fresh cilantro, chopped (optional)

Instructions:

1. **Grill the Corn:**
    - Preheat the grill to medium-high heat. Grill the corn for about 10-12 minutes, turning occasionally, until lightly charred and tender.
2. **Season the Corn:**
    - Brush the grilled corn with melted butter. Sprinkle with chili powder, salt, and pepper. Squeeze fresh lime juice over the top.
3. **Serve:**
    - Garnish with chopped cilantro and serve immediately.

Shrimp Cocktail with Cocktail Sauce

Ingredients:

- 1 lb large shrimp, peeled and deveined
- 1 lemon, quartered
- 1 tablespoon Old Bay seasoning
- 1 cup cocktail sauce
- Fresh parsley for garnish

Instructions:

1. **Cook the Shrimp:**
    - Bring a large pot of water to a boil. Add lemon quarters and Old Bay seasoning. Add shrimp and cook for 2-3 minutes until pink and opaque. Remove the shrimp and set aside to cool.
2. **Prepare the Cocktail Sauce:**
    - Serve the shrimp chilled with cocktail sauce on the side for dipping.
3. **Serve:**
    - Garnish with fresh parsley and serve on a platter or in individual bowls.

Watermelon and Feta Salad

Ingredients:

- 4 cups watermelon, cubed
- 1 cup feta cheese, crumbled
- 1/4 cup fresh mint leaves, chopped
- 2 tablespoons olive oil
- 1 tablespoon balsamic glaze or vinegar
- Salt and pepper to taste

Instructions:

1. **Combine the Ingredients:**
   - In a large bowl, combine the watermelon, crumbled feta cheese, and chopped mint.
2. **Dress the Salad:**
   - Drizzle with olive oil and balsamic glaze. Season with salt and pepper to taste.
3. **Serve:**
   - Toss gently and serve chilled as a refreshing side dish.

Crab Cakes with Remoulade Sauce

Ingredients:

For the Crab Cakes:

- 1 lb lump crab meat, drained and picked over
- 1/2 cup breadcrumbs
- 2 tablespoons mayonnaise
- 1 tablespoon Dijon mustard
- 1 tablespoon fresh parsley, chopped
- 1/2 teaspoon Old Bay seasoning
- 1 egg
- 1 tablespoon lemon juice
- 2 tablespoons olive oil (for frying)

For the Remoulade Sauce:

- 1/2 cup mayonnaise
- 1 tablespoon Dijon mustard
- 1 tablespoon ketchup
- 1 tablespoon lemon juice
- 1 teaspoon hot sauce
- 1 teaspoon capers, chopped
- 1 tablespoon fresh parsley, chopped

Instructions:

1. **Prepare the Crab Cakes:**
   - In a bowl, combine crab meat, breadcrumbs, mayonnaise, mustard, parsley, Old Bay seasoning, egg, and lemon juice. Mix gently until just combined.
2. **Form the Crab Cakes:**
   - Shape the mixture into small patties. Heat olive oil in a skillet over medium heat and cook the crab cakes for 3-4 minutes per side until golden brown and crispy.
3. **Make the Remoulade Sauce:**
   - In a separate bowl, combine mayonnaise, Dijon mustard, ketchup, lemon juice, hot sauce, capers, and parsley. Stir until smooth.
4. **Serve:**

- Serve the crab cakes with remoulade sauce on the side.

Caprese Salad Skewers

Ingredients:

- 1 pint cherry tomatoes
- 1 ball fresh mozzarella, cut into small cubes
- Fresh basil leaves
- 2 tablespoons balsamic glaze
- Salt and pepper to taste
- Skewers or toothpicks

Instructions:

1. **Assemble the Skewers:**
    - Thread a cherry tomato, a basil leaf, and a cube of mozzarella onto each skewer or toothpick.
2. **Season the Skewers:**
    - Drizzle the skewers with balsamic glaze and sprinkle with salt and pepper.
3. **Serve:**
    - Serve immediately as an appetizer or side dish.

Grilled Veggie Kebabs

Ingredients:

- 1 red bell pepper, cut into chunks
- 1 yellow bell pepper, cut into chunks
- 1 zucchini, sliced
- 1 red onion, cut into chunks
- 8 oz mushrooms, halved
- 2 tablespoons olive oil
- 1 teaspoon garlic powder
- 1 teaspoon dried oregano
- Salt and pepper to taste
- Skewers

Instructions:

1. **Prepare the Veggies:**
    - Toss the bell peppers, zucchini, onion, and mushrooms in olive oil, garlic powder, oregano, salt, and pepper.
2. **Assemble the Kebabs:**
    - Thread the vegetables onto the skewers.
3. **Grill the Kebabs:**
    - Preheat the grill to medium-high heat. Grill the vegetable skewers for 8-10 minutes, turning occasionally, until tender and slightly charred.
4. **Serve:**
    - Serve the grilled veggie kebabs immediately as a side dish.

Pineapple Salsa with Tortilla Chips

Ingredients:

- 1 ripe pineapple, diced
- 1/2 red onion, finely chopped
- 1/4 cup fresh cilantro, chopped
- 1 jalapeño, deseeded and finely chopped
- Juice of 1 lime
- Salt to taste
- Tortilla chips for serving

Instructions:

1. **Prepare the Salsa:**
    - In a bowl, combine diced pineapple, red onion, cilantro, jalapeño, and lime juice. Stir to combine.
2. **Season the Salsa:**
    - Season with salt to taste.
3. **Serve:**
    - Serve the pineapple salsa with tortilla chips as a refreshing dip.

Pulled Pork Sliders

Ingredients:

- 2 lbs pork shoulder or butt
- 1 tablespoon olive oil
- 1 onion, chopped
- 1 cup BBQ sauce
- 8 slider buns
- Pickles (optional)
- Coleslaw (optional)

Instructions:

1. **Cook the Pork:**
    - Heat olive oil in a large pot over medium heat. Brown the pork shoulder on all sides. Add chopped onion and cook for a few more minutes.
2. **Simmer:**
    - Add BBQ sauce and 1 cup of water to the pot. Cover and simmer for 2-3 hours, or until the pork is tender and easily shredded.
3. **Shred the Pork:**
    - Remove the pork from the pot and shred it with two forks.
4. **Assemble the Sliders:**
    - Spoon the pulled pork onto slider buns. Add pickles and coleslaw if desired.
5. **Serve:**
    - Serve the sliders warm as a delicious snack or meal.

Guava BBQ Chicken Wings

Ingredients:

- 12 chicken wings
- 1/4 cup guava jelly
- 1/4 cup BBQ sauce
- 1 tablespoon soy sauce
- 1 tablespoon fresh lime juice
- 1 teaspoon garlic powder
- Salt and pepper to taste

Instructions:

1. **Cook the Chicken Wings:**
    - Preheat the oven to 400°F (200°C). Season the chicken wings with salt, pepper, and garlic powder. Bake for 25-30 minutes until crispy and golden.
2. **Prepare the BBQ Sauce:**
    - In a saucepan, combine guava jelly, BBQ sauce, soy sauce, and lime juice. Heat over medium heat until the sauce is smooth and warm.
3. **Coat the Wings:**
    - Toss the baked chicken wings in the guava BBQ sauce.
4. **Serve:**
    - Serve the wings immediately with extra sauce on the side.

Cucumber and Cream Cheese Sandwiches

Ingredients:

- 1 cucumber, thinly sliced
- 8 oz cream cheese, softened
- 1 tablespoon fresh dill, chopped
- 1 tablespoon fresh chives, chopped
- 1 tablespoon lemon juice
- Salt and pepper to taste
- 8 slices of white or whole grain bread (crusts removed)

Instructions:

1. **Prepare the Cream Cheese Spread:**
   - In a bowl, mix the softened cream cheese with chopped dill, chives, lemon juice, salt, and pepper.
2. **Assemble the Sandwiches:**
   - Spread a generous layer of cream cheese mixture onto each slice of bread. Layer with cucumber slices.
3. **Serve:**
   - Place the sandwich slices together, then cut into halves or quarters. Serve chilled or at room temperature.

Roasted Red Pepper and Goat Cheese Dip

Ingredients:

- 2 roasted red peppers, peeled and chopped
- 4 oz goat cheese
- 1/2 cup sour cream
- 2 tablespoons olive oil
- 1 tablespoon lemon juice
- 1 clove garlic, minced
- Salt and pepper to taste

Instructions:

1. **Blend the Ingredients:**
    - In a food processor, combine the roasted red peppers, goat cheese, sour cream, olive oil, lemon juice, and garlic. Blend until smooth.
2. **Season:**
    - Taste and season with salt and pepper as needed.
3. **Serve:**
    - Serve the dip with crackers, pita chips, or fresh veggies.

Hawaiian BBQ Pork Tacos

Ingredients:

- 1 lb pork shoulder
- 1/2 cup BBQ sauce
- 1/2 cup pineapple chunks
- 1 tablespoon soy sauce
- 1 tablespoon brown sugar
- 8 small soft tortillas
- Fresh cilantro, chopped (for garnish)
- Lime wedges (for serving)

Instructions:

1. **Cook the Pork:**
   - Slow-cook the pork shoulder with BBQ sauce, pineapple chunks, soy sauce, and brown sugar for 6-8 hours on low, or until the pork is tender and shreddable.
2. **Shred the Pork:**
   - Shred the cooked pork with two forks and toss it in the sauce mixture.
3. **Assemble the Tacos:**
   - Warm the tortillas and fill them with the shredded BBQ pork. Garnish with fresh cilantro.
4. **Serve:**
   - Serve the tacos with lime wedges on the side.

Mini Fish and Chips Bites

Ingredients:

- 1 lb white fish fillets (such as cod or tilapia), cut into small pieces
- 1 cup flour
- 1 teaspoon baking powder
- Salt and pepper to taste
- 1/2 cup cold sparkling water
- Vegetable oil for frying
- 2 cups frozen fries or homemade fries, cooked and cut into bite-sized pieces
- Tartar sauce (for serving)

Instructions:

1. **Prepare the Batter:**
   - In a bowl, whisk together flour, baking powder, salt, and pepper. Gradually add the sparkling water until you have a smooth batter.
2. **Fry the Fish:**
   - Heat oil in a deep fryer or large pot. Dip the fish pieces into the batter and fry until golden brown, about 3-4 minutes. Remove and drain on paper towels.
3. **Assemble the Bites:**
   - Arrange the fried fish pieces on a platter with bite-sized pieces of cooked fries.
4. **Serve:**
   - Serve the mini fish and chips bites with tartar sauce on the side.

Chips and Salsa

Ingredients:

- 1 bag tortilla chips
- 3 tomatoes, diced
- 1/2 red onion, finely chopped
- 1 jalapeño, deseeded and finely chopped
- 1/4 cup fresh cilantro, chopped
- Juice of 1 lime
- Salt to taste

Instructions:

1. **Make the Salsa:**
    - In a bowl, combine the diced tomatoes, red onion, jalapeño, cilantro, and lime juice. Season with salt to taste.
2. **Serve:**
    - Serve the salsa with tortilla chips for dipping.

Shrimp Ceviche

Ingredients:

- 1 lb shrimp, peeled, deveined, and chopped into small pieces
- Juice of 4 limes
- 1/2 red onion, finely chopped
- 1 tomato, diced
- 1/2 cucumber, peeled and diced
- 1/4 cup fresh cilantro, chopped
- 1 jalapeño, deseeded and finely chopped (optional)
- Salt and pepper to taste

Instructions:

1. **Prepare the Shrimp:**
    - In a bowl, combine the chopped shrimp and lime juice. Let sit for about 30-45 minutes until the shrimp is "cooked" by the lime juice (it will turn pink).
2. **Combine the Ingredients:**
    - Add the red onion, tomato, cucumber, cilantro, and jalapeño to the shrimp. Mix well.
3. **Season and Serve:**
    - Season with salt and pepper to taste. Serve with tortilla chips or on its own.

Grilled Zucchini and Squash

Ingredients:

- 2 zucchinis, sliced into rounds
- 2 yellow squashes, sliced into rounds
- 2 tablespoons olive oil
- 1 teaspoon garlic powder
- Salt and pepper to taste
- Fresh basil, chopped (for garnish)

Instructions:

1. **Prepare the Vegetables:**
    - Toss the zucchini and squash slices with olive oil, garlic powder, salt, and pepper.
2. **Grill the Vegetables:**
    - Preheat the grill to medium heat. Grill the vegetables for 4-5 minutes per side, until tender and slightly charred.
3. **Serve:**
    - Garnish with chopped fresh basil and serve as a side dish.

Chicken Caesar Salad Wraps

Ingredients:

- 2 cups cooked chicken, shredded or sliced
- 4 large flour tortillas
- 2 cups romaine lettuce, chopped
- 1/2 cup Caesar dressing
- 1/4 cup grated Parmesan cheese
- Croutons (optional)

Instructions:

1. **Prepare the Salad:**
    - In a bowl, toss the lettuce, chicken, Caesar dressing, and Parmesan cheese until well combined.
2. **Assemble the Wraps:**
    - Lay out the tortillas and fill them with the Caesar salad mixture. Add croutons if desired.
3. **Serve:**
    - Roll up the tortillas and serve as wraps.

Fresh Fruit Skewers

Ingredients:

- 1 cup strawberries, hulled
- 1 cup pineapple chunks
- 1 cup grapes
- 1 banana, sliced
- 1 cup melon, cubed (such as cantaloupe or watermelon)
- Wooden skewers

Instructions:

1. **Prepare the Fruit:**
   - Cut all the fruit into bite-sized pieces.
2. **Assemble the Skewers:**
   - Thread the fruit onto the skewers, alternating different fruits.
3. **Serve:**
   - Serve the fruit skewers as a refreshing appetizer or snack.

Bacon-Wrapped Dates

Ingredients:

- 16 Medjool dates, pitted
- 8 slices bacon, cut in half
- 1/4 cup goat cheese or cream cheese (optional)
- 1/4 cup toasted almonds (optional)

Instructions:

1. **Prepare the Dates:**
   - If using, stuff each date with a small amount of goat cheese or cream cheese. You can also add a toasted almond inside for extra crunch.
2. **Wrap with Bacon:**
   - Wrap each stuffed date with a half slice of bacon and secure it with a toothpick.
3. **Cook:**
   - Preheat the oven to 375°F (190°C). Place the bacon-wrapped dates on a baking sheet and bake for 20-25 minutes, turning once, until the bacon is crispy.
4. **Serve:**
   - Serve warm as an appetizer.

Beef Sliders with Pickles

Ingredients:

- 1 lb ground beef (80% lean)
- Salt and pepper to taste
- 8 slider buns
- 1/2 cup sliced pickles
- 1 tablespoon olive oil
- Optional toppings: cheese, lettuce, tomato, ketchup, mustard

Instructions:

1. **Prepare the Patties:**
    - Season the ground beef with salt and pepper. Divide it into 8 equal portions and form small patties.
2. **Cook the Sliders:**
    - Heat olive oil in a skillet over medium-high heat. Cook the patties for 3-4 minutes per side, until browned and cooked through.
3. **Assemble the Sliders:**
    - Toast the slider buns lightly. Place a cooked patty on each bun and top with sliced pickles and any other desired toppings.
4. **Serve:**
    - Serve the sliders immediately while hot.

Spicy Tuna Tartare

Ingredients:

- 1/2 lb sushi-grade tuna, finely diced
- 1 tablespoon soy sauce
- 1 tablespoon sesame oil
- 1 teaspoon sriracha (adjust to taste)
- 1 tablespoon green onions, finely chopped
- 1 tablespoon sesame seeds
- 1/4 avocado, diced
- 1/2 cucumber, julienned (optional)
- Wonton chips or crackers for serving

Instructions:

1. **Prepare the Tuna:**
   - In a bowl, combine the tuna, soy sauce, sesame oil, and sriracha. Mix well.
2. **Add Toppings:**
   - Gently fold in the green onions, sesame seeds, avocado, and cucumber (if using).
3. **Serve:**
   - Spoon the tartare onto small plates or serve with wonton chips or crackers.

Chips and Guacamole Stuffed Avocados

Ingredients:

- 2 ripe avocados, halved and pitted
- 1 cup tortilla chips, crushed
- 1/2 cup guacamole (store-bought or homemade)
- 1/4 cup fresh cilantro, chopped
- 1 lime, cut into wedges

Instructions:

1. **Prepare the Avocados:**
    - Halve the avocados and remove the pit. Use a spoon to scoop out some of the flesh to create a larger cavity for the filling.
2. **Assemble the Dish:**
    - Fill each avocado half with guacamole and top with crushed tortilla chips for crunch.
3. **Garnish:**
    - Sprinkle with fresh cilantro and serve with lime wedges on the side.

Grilled Pineapple with Brown Sugar

Ingredients:

- 1 pineapple, peeled and cut into rings or wedges
- 1/4 cup brown sugar
- 1/2 teaspoon cinnamon (optional)
- 1 tablespoon butter (optional)

Instructions:

1. **Prepare the Pineapple:**
    - Preheat the grill to medium heat. Brush the pineapple rings with melted butter, if using.
2. **Grill the Pineapple:**
    - Place the pineapple on the grill and cook for 2-3 minutes per side until grill marks appear and the fruit softens.
3. **Caramelize with Sugar:**
    - Sprinkle brown sugar and cinnamon (if using) over the pineapple during the last minute of grilling.
4. **Serve:**
    - Serve the grilled pineapple warm as a side or dessert.

Bruschetta with Tomato and Basil

Ingredients:

- 1 loaf baguette, sliced into 1/2-inch slices
- 2 large tomatoes, diced
- 1/4 cup fresh basil, chopped
- 2 cloves garlic, minced
- 2 tablespoons olive oil
- 1 tablespoon balsamic vinegar
- Salt and pepper to taste

Instructions:

1. **Toast the Baguette:**
    - Preheat the oven to 400°F (200°C). Place the baguette slices on a baking sheet and toast for 5-7 minutes until golden.
2. **Prepare the Topping:**
    - In a bowl, combine the diced tomatoes, basil, garlic, olive oil, and balsamic vinegar. Season with salt and pepper.
3. **Assemble the Bruschetta:**
    - Spoon the tomato mixture onto the toasted baguette slices.
4. **Serve:**
    - Serve immediately as an appetizer.

Lobster Roll Sliders

Ingredients:

- 1 lb cooked lobster meat, chopped
- 1/4 cup mayonnaise
- 1 tablespoon lemon juice
- 1 tablespoon fresh chives, chopped
- 1/2 teaspoon Old Bay seasoning (optional)
- 8 slider buns
- 1 tablespoon melted butter

Instructions:

1. **Prepare the Lobster Filling:**
   - In a bowl, combine the lobster meat, mayonnaise, lemon juice, chives, and Old Bay seasoning. Mix well.
2. **Assemble the Sliders:**
   - Lightly butter the slider buns and toast them until golden brown. Fill each bun with the lobster mixture.
3. **Serve:**
   - Serve the lobster roll sliders immediately.

Veggie Spring Rolls with Peanut Dipping Sauce

Ingredients for Spring Rolls:

- 8 rice paper wrappers
- 1 cup shredded cabbage
- 1/2 cucumber, julienned
- 1/2 bell pepper, julienned
- 1/4 cup fresh cilantro leaves
- 1/4 cup fresh mint leaves
- 1/4 cup shredded carrots

Ingredients for Peanut Dipping Sauce:

- 1/4 cup peanut butter
- 2 tablespoons soy sauce
- 1 tablespoon rice vinegar
- 1 teaspoon honey
- 1/2 teaspoon sriracha (optional)
- Water to thin

Instructions:

1. **Prepare the Spring Rolls:**
    - Dip a rice paper wrapper in warm water for 5-10 seconds until softened. Lay the wrapper on a clean surface and layer with cabbage, cucumber, bell pepper, cilantro, mint, and carrots.
2. **Roll the Spring Rolls:**
    - Fold in the sides of the wrapper and roll it tightly, like a burrito.
3. **Prepare the Peanut Sauce:**
    - In a small bowl, whisk together the peanut butter, soy sauce, rice vinegar, honey, and sriracha (if using). Add water to thin to your desired consistency.
4. **Serve:**
    - Serve the spring rolls with peanut dipping sauce on the side.

Crab Dip with Crackers

Ingredients:

- 8 oz cream cheese, softened
- 1/2 cup mayonnaise
- 1 tablespoon Dijon mustard
- 1 teaspoon Worcestershire sauce
- 1 teaspoon hot sauce (optional)
- 1/2 cup grated Parmesan cheese
- 1/2 cup shredded mozzarella cheese
- 1 lb lump crab meat, drained and picked through
- 2 tablespoons fresh parsley, chopped
- Salt and pepper to taste
- Assorted crackers for serving

Instructions:

1. **Prepare the Dip:**
    - In a mixing bowl, combine the cream cheese, mayonnaise, Dijon mustard, Worcestershire sauce, hot sauce, Parmesan cheese, and mozzarella cheese. Stir until smooth.
2. **Add the Crab:**
    - Gently fold in the lump crab meat, being careful not to break up the chunks. Season with salt and pepper.
3. **Bake:**
    - Preheat the oven to 375°F (190°C). Transfer the mixture to a baking dish and bake for 20-25 minutes until bubbly and golden on top.
4. **Serve:**
    - Garnish with fresh parsley and serve with crackers.

Mahi-Mahi Tacos with Slaw

Ingredients for Tacos:

- 4 mahi-mahi fillets
- 1 tablespoon olive oil
- 1 teaspoon cumin
- 1 teaspoon chili powder
- Salt and pepper to taste
- 8 small flour tortillas

Ingredients for Slaw:

- 2 cups shredded cabbage
- 1/4 cup shredded carrots
- 1/4 cup cilantro, chopped
- 1 tablespoon lime juice
- 1 tablespoon apple cider vinegar
- Salt and pepper to taste

Instructions:

1. **Prepare the Slaw:**
    - In a bowl, combine the shredded cabbage, carrots, and cilantro. Toss with lime juice, apple cider vinegar, and season with salt and pepper. Set aside to marinate.
2. **Cook the Mahi-Mahi:**
    - Rub the mahi-mahi fillets with olive oil, cumin, chili powder, salt, and pepper. Heat a skillet over medium-high heat and cook the fillets for 3-4 minutes per side until cooked through.
3. **Assemble the Tacos:**
    - Warm the tortillas in a skillet or microwave. Flake the cooked mahi-mahi into the tortillas and top with the slaw.
4. **Serve:**
    - Serve the tacos immediately, optionally garnished with extra cilantro or lime wedges.

BBQ Chicken Drumsticks

Ingredients:

- 12 chicken drumsticks
- 1/4 cup olive oil
- 1 tablespoon garlic powder
- 1 tablespoon paprika
- 1 teaspoon salt
- 1/2 teaspoon black pepper
- 1 cup barbecue sauce

Instructions:

1. **Prepare the Drumsticks:**
    - Preheat the oven to 400°F (200°C). Pat the chicken drumsticks dry with paper towels.
2. **Season the Drumsticks:**
    - In a bowl, mix olive oil, garlic powder, paprika, salt, and pepper. Rub this mixture all over the chicken drumsticks.
3. **Bake:**
    - Arrange the drumsticks on a baking sheet and bake for 35-40 minutes, turning halfway through, until golden and crispy.
4. **Glaze with BBQ Sauce:**
    - Brush the drumsticks with barbecue sauce during the last 5 minutes of baking.
5. **Serve:**
    - Serve the BBQ chicken drumsticks hot with extra sauce on the side.

Baked Mozzarella Sticks

Ingredients:

- 12 mozzarella cheese sticks, cut in half
- 1/2 cup all-purpose flour
- 2 eggs, beaten
- 1 cup breadcrumbs (preferably panko)
- 1/2 cup grated Parmesan cheese
- 1 teaspoon dried oregano
- 1 teaspoon garlic powder
- Salt and pepper to taste
- Marinara sauce for dipping

Instructions:

1. **Prepare the Breading:**
    - Preheat the oven to 400°F (200°C). Set up three shallow bowls: one with flour, one with beaten eggs, and one with breadcrumbs mixed with Parmesan cheese, oregano, garlic powder, salt, and pepper.
2. **Coat the Mozzarella:**
    - Dip each mozzarella stick into the flour, then the egg, and finally coat it with the breadcrumb mixture. Place the coated mozzarella sticks on a baking sheet.
3. **Bake:**
    - Bake for 10-12 minutes until golden and crispy, flipping halfway through.
4. **Serve:**
    - Serve with marinara sauce for dipping.

Pita Bread with Baba Ganoush

Ingredients for Baba Ganoush:

- 2 large eggplants
- 1/4 cup tahini
- 2 tablespoons olive oil
- 1 tablespoon lemon juice
- 2 cloves garlic, minced
- Salt and pepper to taste
- 1 tablespoon fresh parsley, chopped (optional)

Ingredients for Pita Bread:

- 6 pieces pita bread, cut into wedges

Instructions:

1. **Roast the Eggplants:**
   - Preheat the oven to 400°F (200°C). Prick the eggplants with a fork and place them on a baking sheet. Roast for 30-40 minutes until the skin is charred and the flesh is soft.
2. **Prepare the Baba Ganoush:**
   - Once the eggplants are cool enough to handle, peel the skin off and scoop out the flesh. Combine the flesh in a food processor with tahini, olive oil, lemon juice, garlic, salt, and pepper. Process until smooth.
3. **Toast the Pita Bread:**
   - Cut pita bread into wedges and toast or bake until crispy.
4. **Serve:**
   - Serve the baba ganoush with warm pita bread wedges. Garnish with fresh parsley, if desired.

Stuffed Mushrooms

Ingredients:

- 16 large button mushrooms, stems removed
- 1/2 cup cream cheese, softened
- 1/4 cup grated Parmesan cheese
- 2 cloves garlic, minced
- 1/4 cup breadcrumbs
- 2 tablespoons fresh parsley, chopped
- Salt and pepper to taste

Instructions:

1. **Prepare the Mushrooms:**
    - Preheat the oven to 375°F (190°C). Remove the stems from the mushrooms and chop them finely.
2. **Make the Filling:**
    - In a bowl, mix together the chopped mushroom stems, cream cheese, Parmesan, garlic, breadcrumbs, parsley, salt, and pepper.
3. **Stuff the Mushrooms:**
    - Spoon the filling into each mushroom cap.
4. **Bake:**
    - Arrange the stuffed mushrooms on a baking sheet and bake for 15-20 minutes until golden and bubbly.
5. **Serve:**
    - Serve warm as an appetizer.

Poke Nachos

Ingredients:

- 1 lb sushi-grade tuna, diced
- 1/4 cup soy sauce
- 1 tablespoon sesame oil
- 1 teaspoon sriracha (optional)
- 1/2 cup avocado, diced
- 1/4 cup cucumber, julienned
- 1/4 cup radishes, thinly sliced
- 1/2 cup crispy wonton chips
- 1 tablespoon sesame seeds
- 1 tablespoon green onions, chopped

Instructions:

1. **Prepare the Tuna:**
    - In a bowl, combine the tuna with soy sauce, sesame oil, and sriracha. Let it marinate for 10-15 minutes.
2. **Assemble the Nachos:**
    - On a platter, spread the crispy wonton chips. Top with marinated tuna, avocado, cucumber, radishes, sesame seeds, and green onions.
3. **Serve:**
    - Serve immediately as a fun appetizer or snack.

Salmon Croquettes

Ingredients:

- 2 cups cooked salmon, flaked
- 1/2 cup breadcrumbs
- 1/4 cup mayonnaise
- 1 tablespoon Dijon mustard
- 1 tablespoon fresh dill, chopped
- 1 egg, beaten
- Salt and pepper to taste
- Olive oil for frying

Instructions:

1. **Make the Mixture:**
    - In a bowl, combine the flaked salmon, breadcrumbs, mayonnaise, mustard, dill, egg, salt, and pepper. Mix well.
2. **Form the Croquettes:**
    - Shape the mixture into small patties, about 2-3 inches in diameter.
3. **Fry the Croquettes:**
    - Heat olive oil in a skillet over medium heat. Fry the croquettes for 3-4 minutes per side, until golden brown and crispy.
4. **Serve:**
    - Serve the salmon croquettes with a dipping sauce or salad.

Sweet Potato Fries with Ketchup

Ingredients:

- 2 large sweet potatoes, peeled and cut into fries
- 2 tablespoons olive oil
- 1 teaspoon paprika
- 1/2 teaspoon garlic powder
- Salt and pepper to taste
- 1/2 cup ketchup, for dipping

Instructions:

1. **Preheat Oven:**
    - Preheat the oven to 425°F (220°C). Line a baking sheet with parchment paper.
2. **Prepare the Fries:**
    - In a bowl, toss the sweet potato fries with olive oil, paprika, garlic powder, salt, and pepper until evenly coated.
3. **Bake the Fries:**
    - Spread the fries in a single layer on the baking sheet. Bake for 25-30 minutes, flipping halfway through, until crispy and golden brown.
4. **Serve:**
    - Serve the sweet potato fries hot with ketchup on the side for dipping.

Margarita Shrimp Salad

Ingredients:

- 1 lb cooked shrimp, peeled and deveined
- 1 cup cherry tomatoes, halved
- 1 cucumber, diced
- 1/4 cup fresh basil, chopped
- 1/4 cup red onion, thinly sliced
- 2 tablespoons olive oil
- 1 tablespoon balsamic vinegar
- 1 teaspoon lemon juice
- Salt and pepper to taste

Instructions:

1. **Prepare the Salad:**
    - In a large bowl, combine the cooked shrimp, cherry tomatoes, cucumber, basil, and red onion.
2. **Make the Dressing:**
    - In a small bowl, whisk together the olive oil, balsamic vinegar, lemon juice, salt, and pepper.
3. **Toss and Serve:**
    - Pour the dressing over the salad and toss gently to combine. Serve immediately or refrigerate until ready to serve.

Cold Shrimp Salad with Dill and Lemon

Ingredients:

- 1 lb cooked shrimp, peeled and deveined
- 1/2 cup Greek yogurt
- 2 tablespoons mayonnaise
- 1 tablespoon Dijon mustard
- 1 tablespoon fresh dill, chopped
- 1 teaspoon lemon juice
- Salt and pepper to taste
- 1/4 cup celery, diced

Instructions:

1. **Prepare the Salad:**
   - In a large bowl, combine the cooked shrimp, Greek yogurt, mayonnaise, Dijon mustard, dill, lemon juice, salt, and pepper.
2. **Add the Celery:**
   - Fold in the diced celery for crunch and flavor.
3. **Chill and Serve:**
   - Chill the salad for 30 minutes before serving. Serve with crackers or in a lettuce wrap.

Baked Brie with Fig Jam

Ingredients:

- 1 wheel of Brie cheese (8 oz)
- 1/4 cup fig jam
- 1 tablespoon fresh thyme, chopped (optional)
- Crackers or baguette slices for serving

Instructions:

1. **Preheat Oven:**
    - Preheat the oven to 350°F (175°C). Place the Brie cheese wheel on a baking sheet lined with parchment paper.
2. **Prepare the Brie:**
    - Cut a small slit in the top of the Brie and spoon the fig jam over the top. Sprinkle with fresh thyme if using.
3. **Bake the Brie:**
    - Bake for 10-15 minutes, until the Brie is soft and melted.
4. **Serve:**
    - Serve with crackers or sliced baguette for dipping into the gooey, fig-topped cheese.

Grilled Asparagus with Balsamic Glaze

Ingredients:

- 1 bunch asparagus, trimmed
- 1 tablespoon olive oil
- Salt and pepper to taste
- 2 tablespoons balsamic vinegar
- 1 teaspoon honey (optional)

Instructions:

1. **Grill the Asparagus:**
    - Preheat the grill to medium-high heat. Drizzle the asparagus with olive oil and season with salt and pepper. Grill the asparagus for 3-4 minutes, turning occasionally, until tender and slightly charred.
2. **Make the Balsamic Glaze:**
    - In a small saucepan, combine the balsamic vinegar and honey (if using). Simmer over medium heat for 5-7 minutes, until the glaze thickens.
3. **Serve:**
    - Drizzle the balsamic glaze over the grilled asparagus and serve immediately.

Tofu Skewers with Soy Sauce

Ingredients:

- 1 block firm tofu, drained and cubed
- 2 tablespoons soy sauce
- 1 tablespoon sesame oil
- 1 teaspoon rice vinegar
- 1 tablespoon honey or maple syrup
- 1/2 teaspoon garlic powder
- 1/4 teaspoon ground ginger
- 1 tablespoon sesame seeds (optional)
- Skewers for grilling

Instructions:

1. **Marinate the Tofu:**
   - In a bowl, combine the soy sauce, sesame oil, rice vinegar, honey, garlic powder, and ginger. Add the tofu cubes and let them marinate for at least 30 minutes.
2. **Prepare the Skewers:**
   - Thread the tofu onto skewers. Preheat a grill or grill pan over medium heat.
3. **Grill the Tofu:**
   - Grill the skewers for 3-4 minutes per side until golden and slightly crispy.
4. **Serve:**
   - Sprinkle with sesame seeds and serve with steamed rice or a side of vegetables.

Lemon and Herb Marinated Olives

Ingredients:

- 2 cups mixed olives (green and black)
- 1 tablespoon olive oil
- 1 teaspoon lemon zest
- 1 tablespoon lemon juice
- 1 tablespoon fresh rosemary, chopped
- 1 tablespoon fresh thyme, chopped
- 1 garlic clove, minced
- 1/4 teaspoon red pepper flakes (optional)

Instructions:

1. **Prepare the Marinade:**
   - In a bowl, combine the olive oil, lemon zest, lemon juice, rosemary, thyme, garlic, and red pepper flakes (if using).
2. **Marinate the Olives:**
   - Add the olives to the bowl and toss to coat with the marinade. Let the olives marinate for at least 1 hour (or up to 24 hours for more flavor).
3. **Serve:**
   - Serve the marinated olives as an appetizer or snack.